<u>OBADIAH</u>

Seeing the Nations of the World through His Eyes, Especially the World of Islam

A study guide to approaching Internationals.

By

Rev. Dr. Jamil Sadiq

ISBN: 9798858078906

Thanks go to

Rev. D. Wykenham & G. Martin

For their assistance

In preparation of this manuscript.

.

Intro   **Pg v**

Intro

Obadiah is the smallest book in the Old Testament, with 21 verses. Obadiah is one of the Minor Prophets, and his book is standing traditionally between the books of Amos & Jonah in the Old Testament.

He provides glimpses of the story of a conflict between Israel and Edom – the descendants of Abraham's son Isaac. Jacob [the father of Israelites] and Esau, [was also known as Edom and the father of Edomites] were twin brethren. We see the narrative of this conflict in detail in Genesis.

The message that this book contains expresses the importance of brotherhood. God spoke directly to Edom and condemned him for the enmity that he showed to the Israelites. But, unfortunately, Edom ignored the brotherhood, showed hatred and hostility, and refused to love his brother Jacob.

The vision that was seen, and narrated by prophet Obadiah, showed the picture of the hatred of Esau towards his brother Jacob – the children of the Israelites vividly. Edom's abhorrence towards his brother called a spade a spade and showed how callous he was. Everything was clear; his unfeeling approach, uncaring behavior, and insensitive attitude that he performed against Israel hid nothing.

Edom's actions were horrible and straightforwardly an

insult to brotherhood. These actions reflect the ruthless, brutal, vicious, and inhuman stance toward his brother.

God declared that Edom would be accountable for her cruelty and callousness! So we see Edom's role and an accentuated picture of God's judgment in this connection. The Israelites faced tribulation by their adversaries, and Edom refused to take responsibility for taking a stand for Israel!

Edom didn't take this matter seriously, and this act showed her arrogant attitude. So, God revealed to His prophet Obadiah that Edom's destruction was decreed and would take place because of her pride and alliance with Israel's adversaries.

God stated that Israel would be restored. It does also speak about the day of the Lord for all nations. (v.15)

OBADIAH

Seeing the Nations of the World Through His Eyes, Especially the world of Islam

Why do I choose this title for the book of Obadiah? I choose this from Obadiah's declaration. Obadiah is transparently clear that his declaration is for all nations! Edom stands symbolically for all world powers that show hostility toward God and His Christ. All the world's nations that mirror aggression or abhorrence to accept God's plan to redeem nations through Jesus' sacrifice are expressing HCEdom's mindset.

God declares straightforwardly in verses 15,16:

The day of the LORD is near for all nations. As you have done it
will be done to you;
Your deed will return upon your own head.
Just as you drank on my holy hill,
So all the nations will drink continually;
They will drink and drink
And be as if they had never been.
What has been done by the nations?

Rejection and denial of the LORD's Anointed One!
People, nations, and ethnicities of the world want to trust
their own intellect. They trust their intelligence and
understanding and are not ready to believe in God's grace
that works through Christ's redemptive sacrifice.

The Prophet Jeremiah presents this episode of the cup of
God's wrath enormously:

"This is what the LORD, the God of Israel, said to me: "Take
this cup of the wine of wrath from My hand and make all
the nation I am sending you to drink from it. They will
drink, stagger, and go out of their minds because of the
sword I am sending among them." (Jeremiah 25:15,16
HCSB).

Obadiah speaks about God's judgment that will take place
against the world's nations. Each nation that will stand
against God's Masih, her destiny is determined and set
already.

No nation or people group can escape from this judgment.

How can I claim this?

I can claim this because God's Word declares clearly in Romans 1:19, 'Since what may be known about God is plain to them, because God has made it plain to them.'

People, individually, want to do good deeds or do charitable things. Why? There's some reason: They do these things to attain or avail something for filling out the vacuum of their souls. They are doing it out of their senses and solid consciousness.

Undoubtedly, God created a man and provided him with a gift of a mind. Why did He provide a mind? Simply, so he may have the power and ability to think. He provided man a free will. So, he must choose what is good or bad for him. And God provided him with a conscience too, with which he can define, determine, or decide what decision to make – good or bad.

No one is there who can prove himself innocent concerning sin and rebellion and its tragic consequences. Francis Schaefer in his book **'The God Who Is There.' Says,** "Regardless of a man's system, he has to live in God's world." It is hard for mankind to remove the truth that God has stamped, carved, and imprinted on man's soul.

Still, we see, as it is revealed in Psalms, it is happening all over the world. The world's nations and individuals are living with a rebellious attitude. The Psalmist pours out his worried heart concerning the nations of the world seeing them standing in the defiant and arrogant style against the LORD God. He pens the situation in such a way:

"Why do the nations rebel and the people plot in vain? The kings of the earth take their stand, and the rulers conspire together against the LORD and His Anointed One: "Let us tear off their chains and free ourselves from their restraints." (Psalms "The Zaboor Sharif" 2:1-3)

The Evangelist John mentions in his gospel: "The one who believes in the Son has eternal life, but the one who refuses to believe in the Son will not see life; instead, the wrath of God remains on him." (John "The Injil Sharif" 3:36).

The Lord Jesus Christ delivered His perspective to His disciples: "When the Son of Man comes in His glory, and all the angels with Him, then he will sit on the thrones of his glory. All the nations will be gathered before Him, and He will separate them one from another, just as a shepherd separates the sheep from the goats." (Matthew "Injil Sharif" 25:31-32).

Whoa! What a declaration! The Kingdom will be the LORD's! He is the Sovereign God. Everything in the world is under His Lordship and Kingship! There's no exception available; even the rejecters of faith have to bow down before Him one day.

Obadiah's oracle is not only for Edomites it is for all nations. It is for all nations who consider **"reality is impersonal"** – **that is, straightforwardly denial of the creator God. and for the nations who believe in God but they consider His**

Being as a distant God.

One Islamic creedal statement reads,

"And God Most High is the Creator of all actions of His creatures whether of unbelief or belief, of obedience or of rebellion: all of them are by the will of God and His sentence and his conclusion and His decreeing." [1] (Norman L Geisler& Abdul Saleeb Taken from the Al-Nasfi's creed as cited by Cragg 60-61)

That is utterly opposed to the Judeo-Christian worldview. Isn't it?

And the Word of God is clear:

The day of the LORD is near for all nations. As you have done it will be done to you;

God spoke through His prophet Obadiah to many nations. Can we learn anything about Islam? Well! There's nothing available that speaks directly about the world of Islam, but there are several striking parallels available that can help us to learn about Islam as we go through this tiny book of the Old Testament.

For example, one of the famous poets of the Islamic world presents Muslim people using the imagery of an eagle!

Oh Eagle, don't be despondent
Due to the swift and rough breeze,
For it only blows in this manner
To make you fly faster and higher.
Dr. Iqbal

Edom has a prideful heart because of its abode, which is an indomitable and unassailable rock fortress of the eagle.

Obadiah - the author of this tiny book, the diction of his name helps us to understand who a true Muslim is and the traits of a person who considers himself, and claims to be, a Muslim.

Who are the people who considered themselves adversaries of Israel? Who are those in the world who profess pridefully and declares unashamedly, *"wipe out Israel from the face of the earth."*

Digging deeper into Obadiah's Oracle and the prophecies he delivered can be contemplated keeping in view the context of the present era and the world of Islam!!

Indeed, it has enormous potential!

His,

Jamil Sadiq

Week 1: God's Search for Worshipers

Obadiah:

The slave or worshipper of God?

Week 1:

God's Search for Worshippers

"The vision of Obadiah. This is what the Sovereign LORD says about Edom – "
Obadiah 1:1 (NIV)

The beauty of the Christian God is this: He is the God who pursues people. His heart is after His lost creation. He is not a distant or aloof god. He is YHWH God - the Father who wants to see His children who have gone astray come back to His home and dine at His wonderful table. Because of His amazing beauty and uncontrolled grace, He continues His search for true worshipers.

Background Thoughts

What is the significance of Obadiah's book in the Old Testament? What attracts your attention to this small book?

_____

_____

_____

_____

_____

Do you have any stories to share about dreams or visions? Does God speak through dreams or visions nowadays? What is your perspective on it?

_____

_____

_____

_____

_____

Insight on the Text

Vision: (v.1a) to visualize something in one's senses with the naked eyes

Obadiah: (v.1a) a worshipper or servant of God

Sovereign LORD: (v.1b) the LORD God who is self-sufficient and sustains everything in the universe.

A message from the LORD: (1c) it is not the communication of a king or some influential person but of God.

An Envoy: (1d) a representative or an ambassador to the nations of the world.

The Text
Obadiah 1: 1-9

1. *"The vision of Obadiah.*

   *This is what the Sovereign LORD
   says about Edom –
   We have heard a message from the
   LORD:
   An envoy was sent to the nations to
   say,
   "Rise, let us go against her for battle" –*

Overview of the Word
"Obadiah"

Obadiah: means a servant or a slave of God; a worshipper of Jehovah God.

Let me tell you about the relationship between a slave and the Lord sharing Juan Carlos's story. This story is a beautiful reflection of a slave and a master's relationship. [Adapted from the Disciple Creation House, pp.34-35.]

'A man sees this pearl and says to the merchant,'

Buyer: "I want this pearl. How much is it?"
Seller: The seller says, "It's very expensive." "How much?" "A lot!"
Buyer: "Well, do you think I could buy it?" the man asks
Seller: "Oh, yes," says the merchant, "everyone can buy it."
Buyer: "But I thought you said it was very expensive."
Seller: "I did."
Buyer: "Well, how much?"
Seller: "Everything you have," says the seller.
Buyer: "All right, I'll buy it."
Seller: "Okay, what do you have?"
Buyer: "Well, I have $10,000 in the bank."
Seller: "Good, $10,000. What else?"
Buyer: "That's all I have." "Nothing more?" "Well, I have a few dollars more in my pocket."
Seller: "How much?"
Buyer: "Let's see ... $100."

Seller: "That's mine, too," says the seller.
"What else do you have?" "That's all, nothing else."
"Where do you live?" the seller asks.
Buyer: "In my house. Yes, I own a home."
The seller writes down, "house." "It's mine."
Buyer: "Where do you expect me to sleep—in my camper?"
Seller: "Oh, you have a camper, do you? That, too.
What else"
Buyer: "Am I supposed to sleep in my car?"
Seller: "Oh, you have a car?"
Buyer: "Yes, I own two of them."
Seller: "They're mine now."
Buyer: "Look, you've taken my money, my house, my
camper, and my cars. Where is my family going to live?"
Seller: "So, you have a family?"
Buyer: "Yes, I have a wife and three kids."
Seller: "They're mine now."

[Suddenly the seller exclaims,]

Seller: "Oh, I almost forgot! *You* yourself, too! Everything
becomes mine—wife, children, house, money, cars, and you,
too."

[Then he goes on,]

Seller: "Now, listen, I will allow you to use all these things
for the time being. But don't forget that they're all mine, just
as you are. And whenever I need any of them, you must give
them up, because I am now the owner."

How do we recognize ourselves? Do we recognize ourselves

by our work? Or something else? What is our character or identity? How could you possibly answer it? I have no clue . . . what do you think about it?

Indeed, what we do is something that determines or marks our identity or character.

In a prayer meeting, a sister explained that we are the sheep of His pen. And she was saying, "Sheep are usually considered to be stupid." When delivering these words, she was reluctant to use the word stupid. On noticing, that she was feeling some hesitation in using this word, I interrupted her, "We need not express timidity because this is the very characteristic of sheep."

Being Christians, we do believe we are sheep. But seldom do we want to consider ourselves stupid or foolish. This explanation seems ridiculous to us. We do not want to consider ourselves sheep in this manner. Though this is the straightforward truth from early church history, the message of the cross seems foolish to the intellectual world! (1 Corinthians 1:18)

I am confident the same is with the word "Slave." Considering yourself to be a slave is not a desirable thing. Indisputably considering ourselves to be slaves is foolishness. We do not want to consider ourselves slaves.

In a democratic system, it is not a tolerating act to take or own this title. Still, the great apostle Paul always considered himself a slave. "A Bond-Servant" or "A Slave of Christ" –

the Apostle Paul used this expression as a remarkable title.

"I am obligated both to Greeks and non-Greeks, both to the wise and the foolish. That's why I am so eager to preach the gospel also to you who are in Rome." (Romans 1:14-15 NIV).

God says, *"If I am a Master where is the respect due Me?"* (Malachi 1:6 NIV)[4]

God says, "If I am your Master why don't you show respect to Me?" Can we analyze how many hours or days in a week, or a month we take His word, His Great Commission, or Great Commandment seriously?

An honest analysis of our inner being reveals to us that we are facing this predicament from the innermost recesses of our hearts. We are jammed and in a dilemma; aren't we? We have a number of issues to deal with, uncertainties, and worries to face in our daily lives that compel or pave the way for opening up the windows or doors for qualms, fears, and doubts.

"Does God care about my feelings and hurts?" "Why doesn't God intervene in my situation?" "Where is He now?"
"Is His Word true?"

We have plenty of tough and challenging questions to deal with.

We know Jesus encountered a woman in a town of Samaria called Sychar at Jacob's well at the sixth hour of the day (presently 12:00 noon) to deal with the issues of her life.

She was unrelentingly talking to Jesus, providing insight into Jesus' Prophethood. She brought about the issue of worshipping God on Mount Gerizim – where Abraham and Jacob had built altars (Genesis 12:6-7; 33:18-20).

Jesus enlightens her understanding about worshipping, saying, *"Believe me, woman, an hour is coming when you will worship the Father neither on this mountain nor in Jerusalem. You Samaritans worship what you do not know; we worship what we do know, because salvation is from the Jews. But an hour is coming, and is now here, when the true worshipers will worship the Father in spirit and truth. Yes, the Father wants such people to worship Him. God is Spirit, and those who worship Him must worship in spirit and truth."* (John "Injil Sharif" 4:21-24 HCSB).

He brought out to her attention the debate about the place of worship. He reveals to her that what is most important is whom we worship and not the place where we worship. Are we worshiping God, keeping God's nature in mind, or not? And the most beautiful thing to know is that God Himself is rummaging around, seeking out and searching for true worshipers.

Q1.1 Why did Obadiah start his book with the word "The Vision"? Does this influence people to believe in the authenticity of the declared word?

_____

_____

_____

_____

_____

Q1.2 Edom being a nation, feels secure and safe? Why would they feel this way?

_____

_____

_____

_____

_____

Q1.3 Obadiah used the word "We" in verse 1 of his oracle. Why did he use the word "We"?

_____

_____

_____

_____

_____

Q1.4 Please read Jeremiah 49:14-16. Aren't these verses of the book of Jeremiah parallel to the verses of Obadiah 1-4? Why do you think this is?

_____

_____

_____

_____

_____

Q1.5 We know well that God has been speaking throughout history through dreams and visions in both the Old and New Testaments. Does He speak through these means nowadays? What do you think?

_____

_____

_____

A Link to Islam

Obadiah: The slave or worshipper of God is the first parallel in the book of Obadiah that will help us to understand the Muslim mindset.

A Muslim man considers himself subservient and submissive to Allah – a slave. He bows down before Allah with profound adoration, reverence, and veneration.

Muslims are proud people. They have a solid cultural background and strong social ties in their traditions and Islamic rituals. We can't work among them without grasping their intellectual approach and wit. They have a zeal for their religion at such a level that they are ready to die for it. They don't care what people say or think about them. They have their own agendas and global vision.

These days, we see the reality of suicide attacks, dubbed *terrorism.* We label it *radical Islam, extremism,* or *Islamic fundamentalism.* Have you ever honestly wondered how such people are led to carry on such horrific and cruel acts? Where does this fervent ambition to kill people stem from? Are they crazy or mindless? If we scrutinize Islam and understand its true nature, we will have a better chance of reaching our Muslim friends trapped in Islam.

When I say that we need to study Islam or our Muslim friends, we should not take it incorrectly. We do not intend to raise any resentful or harsh feelings or attitudes towards beloved Muslim friends.

In general, Muslims are innocent, friendly, and hospitable. The reason we study Muslims is to offer Christ to them. And there are plenty of Muslims to go around! Islam is a world religion with more than one billion adherents. One out of every five people in the world is Muslim! Islam dominates multitudes of people politically, socially, and culturally. It rules in more than forty-five Muslim nations, and its roots have reached almost every corner of the earth. It is a world power flavored by many cultures.

The Old Testament talks about the Master and a slave's relationship, but Jesus' perspective is radical and totally opposite to the Old Testament.

Jesus said,

"I no longer call you slaves anymore, because a slave does not know what his master is doing. I have called you friends, because I have made known to you everything I have heard from My Father. You did not choose me, but I chose you. I appointed you that you should go out and produce fruit and that your fruit should remain . . ." (John "Injil Sharif" 15:15-16)

How beautiful!

Jesus stated that we are not servants. Our calling is a higher calling. It is a call to friendship. He called us to be His friends. He himself has chosen us and appointed us to this rank to be His friends.

Glory goes to our Lord!

Hallelujah!

Q1.6 How will you define the word Muslim? Do you know what they believe? (See Appendix A "Islamic faith")

_____

_____

_____

_____

_____

Q1.7 Have you ever encountered a Muslim friend? How was your experience?

_____

_____

_____

_____

_____

Q1.8 God is rummaging around in pursuit of genuine seekers. Being His agent, how can you most easily make a footprint of His grace in a Muslim's heart -- by using the Bible or the Quran? Support your answer with reasoning.

_____

_____

_____

_____

_____

Q1.9 What is the connecting point between the two words "Muslim" & "Obadiah"? In what manner are they similar -- if they are..?

_____

_____

_____

_____

_____

Q1.10 Is it time to introduce the Bible to your Muslim friend? How will you do it?

_____

_____

_____

_____

_____

Q1.11 Obadiah – is a common name in Hebrews with meanings of worshiper or a devotee. (See Ezra 8:9; Nehemiah 10:5; 2 Chronicle 17:7;1Kings 18: 3-16). There are worshipers available in the world religions. Does this matter? Frankly speaking, it does not! What matters the most or what is significantly noteworthy is this: to whom one worships. Write down your thoughts.

_____

_____

_____

_____

_____

_____

_____

_____

_____

Personal Reflection: How should we pray in light of what you just studied this week?

_____

_____

_____

_____

_____

How did God speak to you this week?

_____

_____

_____

_____

_____

_____

_____

_____

_____

_____

_____

_____

_____

_____

_____

_____

Challenging Scenario

How can you play your role to become a partner in YHVH God's search for true worshipers?

_____
_____
_____
_____
_____
_____
_____
_____
_____
_____
_____
_____
_____
_____
_____
_____
_____
_____
_____
_____
_____
_____
_____
_____
_____
_____

Week 2: God's Justice Rules

A declared prediction about

Edom's destruction

Reasons for destruction: Pride

God's Justice Rules

"See, I will make you small among the nations; you will be utterly despised."

Obadiah 1:2 (NIV)

God is the God of Justice. He is, from beginning to end, all through justice. His justice rules from end to end all the way through. He judges righteously without making any distinction.

Background Thoughts

Do you remember when you faced rejection? What was your first reaction? How did you handle it? How do most people react when facing rejection?

_____

_____

_____

_____

_____

How will you handle it when someone reacts in anger or resentment? Does this reflect a cry for justice, or are there other elements involved?

_____

_____

_____

_____

_____

Insight on the Text

Edom: (v.1) a dwelling place or land of Edomites, the descendants of Esau, also known as Idumea.

Ambassador: (v.1) a representative or an envoy.

I have made thee small: (v.2) God's declaration because of Edom's arrogant heart.

Thou art greatly despised: (v.2) totally shunned, hated, and rejected.

Pride: (v.3) is the opposite of humility. It expresses someone's state of arrogance, and it reflects self-importance.

Thou mount on high as the eagle: (v.4) a simile for a prideful attitude.

Though thy nest be set among the stars: (v.4) the highest thoughts to dwell in lofty places.

How are the things of Esau searched: (v.6) Esau will be robbed and looted by his partners and allies.

Thy confederacy have brought thee on the way: Friends of Esau will deceive and overpower. And Edom will face terrible situations at the hands of his friends.

Destroy the wise men out of Edom: (v.8) Edom is reliant on the wisdom of his men—another egotistical and arrogant perspective of Edomites. But God declares that no more wisdom will be available to the people of Edom. Therefore, God will turn over the wisdom of the Edomites.

Thy mighty men: (v.9a) warriors, the brave men, the frontiers, soldiers, and troops.

Teman: (v.9b) Esau's grandson from Eliphaz (See Genesis 36:11).

The Text
Obadiah 1: 2-9 ASV

¹ The vision of Obadiah.

Thus saith the Lord Jehovah concerning Edom: We have heard tidings from Jehovah, and an ambassador is sent among the nations, saying, Arise ye, and let us rise up against her in battle.

² Behold, I have made thee small among the nations: thou art greatly despised.

³ The pride of thy heart hath deceived thee, O thou that dwellest in the clefts of the rock, whose habitation is high; that saith in his heart, Who shall bring me down to the ground?

⁴ Though thou mount on high as the eagle, and though thy nest be set among the stars, I will bring thee down from thence, saith Jehovah.

⁵ If thieves came to thee, if robbers by night (how art thou cut off!), would they not steal only till they had enough? if grape-gatherers came to thee, would they not leave some gleaning grapes?

⁶ How are the things of Esau searched! how are his hidden treasures sought out!

⁷ All the men of thy confederacy have brought thee on thy way, even to the border: the men that were at peace with thee have deceived thee, and prevailed against thee; they that eat thy bread lay a snare under thee: there is no understanding in him.

⁸ Shall I not in that day, saith Jehovah, destroy the wise men out of Edom, and understanding out of the mount of Esau?

⁹ And thy mighty men, O Teman, shall be dismayed, to the end that every one may be cut off from the mount of Esau by slaughter.

Overview of the Character of "Esau "

Esau literally keeps the meaning of "Red." This means the godless son Hebrews 12:16 *"See that no one is sexually immoral, or is godless like Esau, who for a single meal sold his inheritance rights as the oldest son."*

A Declared Prediction about Edom's Destruction And the Reasons for This Enmity!!

God's declaration for Edom started with this announcement, *"Behold, I have made thee small among the nations: thou art greatly despised" (v.2).* And in the next verse, God justifies this announcement against her. He explains a vivid description of her fall. Indeed, the destruction will take place because of her pride.

Pride is the key root of her fall, ruin, and devastation.

How strange it is! Esau chose to fill his empty stomach with red lentils despising his privileges of being the firstborn in the family. This deal was not an ideal deal. Esau's arrogant attitude reflects his stupidity. His character shows up clear-cut; he was dull, not sharp enough to understand what a great asset he has refuted, making such a godless decision! The refutation of his birthright was the refutation of God's grace. God blessed him with the right to be the firstborn, the oldest son, but he sold it for *a single meal.* He trusted his worldly intellect, saying, *"Look, I am about to die," Esau said. "What good is the birthright to me?" (Genesis 25:32 NIV).*

Later, when he realized how significant the loss was that he would face by denying his inheritance right, he tried to fix the issue, and he tried hard, with tears, to restore what he lost, but *"He could bring about no change of mind." (Hebrews 12:17).*
There's indeed no use crying over spilled milk.

This event was the root cause of brotherhood disparity. It opened the door for Jacob's acceptance and Esau's rejection. Esau's lineage is known as Edom (Genesis 36;1) On Moses' request to provide a safe route for the Israelites, the Edomites raised the swords barring their swords, barring the way (Numbers 20).

Let's read the Word of God, Numbers 20:14-21 (NIV).

14. *"Moses sent messengers from Kadesh to the king of Edom, saying: "This is what your brother Israel says: You know about all the hardships that have come upon us.*

15. Our forefathers went down into Egypt, and we lived there many years. The Egyptians mistreated us and our fathers,
16. but when we cried out to the LORD, he heard our cry and sent an angel and brought us out of Egypt. "Now we are here at Kadesh, a town on the edge of your territory.
17. Please let us pass through your country. We will not go through any field or vineyard, or drink water from any well. We will travel along the king's highway and not turn to the right or to the left until we have passed through your territory.
18. But Edom answered:
"You may not pass through here; if you try, we will march out and attack you with the sword."
19. The Israelites replied: "We will go along the main road, and if we or our livestock drink any of your water, we will pay for it. We only want to pass through on foot – nothing else.
20. Again they answered: "You may not pass through." Then Edom came out against them with a large and powerful army.
21. Since Edom refused to let them go through their territory, Israel turned away from them."

Q2.1 Who made this statement, *"we will march out and attack you with the sword."* (v.18)? What resonance would your ears be able to hear? Who are those people who use swords as their pride?

_____

_____

_____

_____

Q2.2 Would it be okay to say Moses' messengers responded well to the King of Edom in v. 19? If yes, then how?

_____

_____

_____

_____

_____

God's declaration to despise Edom totally and utterly takes place because of Edom's arrogant attitude and behavior toward her brother nation Israel (read Ezekiel 35 to see detail). God spoke directly to Edom and condemned him for the enmity that he showed to the Israelites. Edom ignored the brotherhood and showed hatred and enmity, and refused to love his brother Jacob.

The Psalmist entrusts his bitterness concerning the Edomites' cruelty in Psalm 137. His tone is utter, stark, and harsh. He demands God's justice blatantly in favor of the Israelites and says;

"Remember, O LORD, what the Edomites did on the day Jerusalem fell.
"Tear it down," they cried,
"tear it down to its foundation!" (Psalms "the Zaboor Sharif"
137:7 NIV).

All this was taking place because of the ancient hostility – the grudge and conflict developed between two brothers, Jacob and Esau. So we see in the Pentateuch in the book of Numbers when Moses sent a delegate to the King of Edom how harshly he rejected them.

Moses' messengers approached the King of Edom and requested very nicely, bringing to his attention the brotherhood ties between them. They tried hard to remind him that blood is thicker than water by emphasizing Abraham's lineage. They highlighted and pointed out *"forefathers,"* (v.15) so the Edomites would realize the importance of their blood relationship!

So they may grasp the significance of brotherhood!

Unquestionably! It was a brotherly communication with eloquent, humble entreaty, *"Please let us pass through your country. We will not go through any field or vineyard, or drink water from any well. We will travel along the king's highway and not turn to the right or to the left until we have passed through your territory."* (Numbers 20:17)

They sketched out the whole plan by passing through the public road - - the route that has gained its reputation and fame to be called by the people the king's highway. The messengers negotiated, discussed, and elaborated on everything in detail.

They explicitly explained that passing in this way would be totally harmless! No field, vineyard, or well will be misused. They mentioned they would take care by every possible means, not going "to the right or to the left" until they passed through the land!

No doubt, going through the East across the Jordan by passing through the king's road was smooth, safer, and easier to than going through the other side – the south side. Indeed, it would not be considered a good idea by anyone to travel on the South end of Edom because of its *steep and lofty mountain ranges.* Surely, these steeps and mountain ranges could play their role well to produce hardships for the Israelites. So, they were ready to pay for the services they were supposed to receive, on behalf of their community, children, and cattle, on their way crossing the king's road. Yet, their request encountered a harsh response, disappointing feedback, and an arrogant rejection.

Q2.3 Why did the Edomites, the descendant of Esau, refuse to let Israel by passing through their territory?

_____
_____
_____
_____

Q2.4 Do you think Israel had any evil motive behind this entreaty? Wasn't that an excellent bonus package for the economy of the Edomites?

_____
_____
_____
_____
_____

Q2.6 Which highway was mentioned by Moses' messengers for passing through Edom?

_____
_____
_____
_____

Q2.7 How sweet is it? The messengers started their conversation by saying, *"This is what your brother Israel says."* How would you describe their relational approach? Can we dare to address Islamic friends – brothers and sisters? Why yes or why not?

_____

_____

_____

_____

_____

Q2.8 Who advised Israel, *"You are about to pass through the territory of your brothers, the descendants of Esau, who live in Sier. They will be afraid of you, but be very careful. . . "*? (See the reference from the Torah Sharif Deuteronomy 2:4; 2:8: 23:7). Where do you think Islamic friends are standing in God's perspective? Do we need to use a polemic approach to address their issues?

_____

_____

_____

_____

_____

A Link to Islam

Ishmael is the link between Islam and Christianity. Christians recognize the man Ishmael as the son of Abraham by his concubine, Hagar the Egyptian. Abraham was eighty-six years old when Ishmael was born. When the LORD required Abraham to be circumcised, Ishmael was thirteen years old. We can see the Biblical story of Hagar (Hajira) and her son Ishmael in detail in Genesis 16 -17; 25:12-18; 28: 8,9; 36:1-3; 1 Chronicles 1:28-31; Romans 9:7-9; and Galatians 4:21-31.

According to the Bible, Sarah gave her handmaid, Hagar, as a concubine to Abraham (Ibrahim) to be a wife of Abraham to bear a child, according to Eastern cultural tradition. When Hagar realized she had conceived, her attitude toward her mistress Sarah changed immediately. She despised her mistress and became her rival. Because Hagar insulted her, Sarah approached Abraham with a complaint against her. Abraham said, *"Do with her whatever you think is best."* (Genesis 16:6). This encourages Sarah to begin mistreating Hagar. As a result, Hagar had to flee from her. While Hagar was in the wilderness, she encountered an angel of God and was given assurance that she and her son could safely return to Sarah.

God Almighty favored Sarah's decision, and Abraham had to agree with Sarah. Even though Hagar was the mother of Abraham's son, Ishmael, she was not awarded the same status as Sarah in the household. Though the Hebrews rejected her, she found favor with God. God spoke to her two times through his angel and predicted Ishmael's future.

Islamic Belief: A Conflict between Ishmael & Isaac.
According to Islamic beliefs, Abraham (Ibrahim), Hagar, and Ishmael are known as the founding family of the Arab people. The Quran claims that Mecca was the place where Hagar and Ishmael faced a desperate situation without water. This is why part of the Hajj (the pilgrimage to Mecca performed by Muslims) includes walking between two mountains in Mecca and pondering Hagar and Ishmael's story. Read the story through the Hadith (the Book of the Traditions of the Prophet).

Sahih Al-Bukhari 4:584 (The Narration of Ibn 'Abbas)
> When Abraham had differences with his wife (because of her jealousy of Hajira, Ishmael's mother), he took Ishmael and his mother and went away. They had a water-skin with them containing some water. Ishmael's mother used to drink water from the water-skin so that her milk would increase for her child. When Abraham reached Mecca, he made her sit under a tree and afterwards returned home. Ishmael's mother followed him, and when they reached Kaaba, she called him from behind, 'O Abraham! To whom are you leaving us?'
>
> He replied, '(I am leaving you) to Allah's (care).'
>
> She said, 'I am satisfied to be with Allah.' She returned to her place and started drinking water from the water-skin, and her milk increased for her child. When the water had all been used up, she said to

herself, 'I'd better go and look so that I may see somebody.' She ascended Safa Mountain and looked, hoping to see somebody, but in vain. When she came down to the valley, she ran until she reached Marwa Mountain. She ran to and fro (between the two mountains) many times. Then she said to herself, 'I'd better go and see the state of the child.' She went and found (him) in a state of one on the point of dying. She could not endure to watch (him) dying, and said (to herself), 'If I go and look, I may find somebody.' She went and ascended Safa Mountain and looked for a long while but could not find anybody. Thus she completed seven rounds (of running) between Safa and Marwa.

Again she said (to herself), 'I'd better go back and see the state of the child.' But suddenly she heard a voice, and she said to that strange voice, 'Help us if you can offer any help.'

Lo! It was Gabriel (who had made the voice). Gabriel hit the earth with his heel like this (Ibn 'Abbas hit the earth with his heel to Illustrate it), and so the water gushed out. Ishmael's mother was astonished and started digging.

Abu Al-Qasim the Prophet said, "If she had left the water, (flow naturally without her intervention), it would have been flowing on the surface of the earth."

Ishmael's mother started drinking from the water and her milk increased for her child. Afterwards some people of the tribe of Jurhum, while passing through the bottom of the valley, saw some birds, and that astonished them, and they said, 'Birds can only be found at a place where there is water.' They sent a messenger who searched the place and found the water, and returned to inform them about it.

Then they all went to her and said, 'O Ishmael's mother! Will you allow us to be with you (or dwell with you)?' (And thus they stayed there.)

Later on her boy reached the age of puberty and married a lady from them.

Then an idea occurred to Abraham, which he disclosed to his wife (Sarah), 'I want to call on my dependents I left (at Mecca).' When he went there, he greeted (Ishmael's wife) and said, 'Where is Ishmael?'

She replied, 'He has gone out hunting.'

Abraham said (to her), 'When he comes, tell him to change the threshold of his gate.'

When he came, she told him the same; whereupon Ishmael said to her, 'You are the threshold, so go to your family (i.e., you are divorced).'

Again Abraham thought of visiting his dependents whom he had left (at Mecca), and he told his wife (Sarah) of his intentions. Abraham came to Ishmael's house and asked. 'Where is Ishmael?'

Ishmael's wife replied, 'He has gone out hunting,' and added, 'Will you stay (for some time) and have something to eat and drink?'

Abraham asked, 'What is your food and what is your drink?'

She replied, 'Our food is meat and our drink is water.'

He said, 'O Allah! Bless their meals and their drink.'

Abu Al-Qasim the Prophet said, "Because of Abraham's invocation there are blessings (in Mecca)."

Once more Abraham thought of visiting his family he had left (at Mecca), so he told his wife (Sarah) of his decision. He went and found Ishmael behind the Zam-zam well, mending his arrows. He said, 'O Ishmael, Your Lord has ordered me to build a house for Him.'

Ishmael said, 'Obey (the order of) your Lord.'

Abraham said, 'Allah has also ordered me that you should help me therein.'

Ishmael said, 'Then I will do (it).'

So, both of them rose and Abraham started building (the Kaaba) while Ishmael went on handing him the stones, and both of them were saying, 'O our Lord! Accept (this service) from us, Verily, You are the All-Hearing, the All-Knowing.'

When the building became high and the old man (Abraham) could no longer lift the stones (to such a high position), he stood over the stone of Al-Maqam and Ishmael carried on handing him the stones, and both of them were saying, 'O our Lord! Accept (this service) from us, Verily, You are All-Hearing, All-Knowing.' (2.127) [See Appendix (A)]

Q2.9 What challenges had Israel faced when confronted by Edom's denial? How had Moses' messengers summarized for the king of Edom the hardships and hatred they met at the hands of the Egyptians and the faithfulness of YHVH God for providing them redemption from Egypt's slavery?

_____

_____

_____

_____

_____

Q2.10 Can we use our testimonies, even sharing our sufferings and humiliation that we face from our adversary's hands, to explain to our Muslim friends how the faithful God helps to prevail over temptations and many evil things we encounter? How has God, by providing Jesus' grace, made it possible for us to live victorious lives with assurance and confidence in His redemptive work?

_____

_____

_____

_____

_____

Q2.11 How had the Edomites threatened their Israelites' brethren?

_____

_____

_____

_____

_____

Personal Reflection: How should we pray in light of what you just studied this week?

_____

_____

_____

_____

_____

How did God speak to you this week?

_____

_____

_____

_____

_____

_____

_____

_____

_____

_____

Challenging Scenario

What is your plan for this week for reaching Islamic friends? How can we develop a solid strategic plan to help internationals? Would you like to share a few ideas about this?

_____

_____

_____

_____

_____

_____

_____

_____

_____

_____

_____

_____

_____

Week 3: God Cares, Do I?

Why do I stand aloof?

The Brotherhood

Esau's pride and hatred toward Israel vs. Church's Pride and hatred toward the People of the Crescent

Week 3

God Cares, Do I?

"On the day you stood aloof . . . in the day of his misfortune"

Obadiah 1:11-12 (NIV)

Our God cares! This is His beauty. Because of His gracious love and merciful heart, He is caring, compassionate and considerate. No other god(s) in any religion shows care like YHVH God, who gave His only begotten Son to save mankind!

Background Thoughts

Whom do you consider a very caring person in your circle of friends? What characteristics compel you to make this decision about your friend?

_____

_____

_____

_____

_____

Is this easy-going or challenging to take care of others? What is your opinion about this? How can you say that caring is a reflection of gratitude? Does this reflect an action of a grateful heart? How can you say that only a grateful heart expresses this action?

_____

_____

_____

_____

_____

Insight on the Text

Violence: (v.10a) an act of hostility

Covered: (v.10b) something not exposed or opened

Stoodest on the other side: (v.11) standing in the distance. Stood aloof and far away.

Strangers: (v.11) outsiders, aliens.

Cast lots: (v.11) a procedure, method, or practice to discern God's will.

Look not though on the day: (v.12) do not look down, gloat, or throw a contemptuous look, showing a disrespectful attitude.

Enter not: (v.13) Edomites preferred to walk through with the enemies of Israelites to show them their support and that they are with them.

Gates: (v.13) entrances or gateways, specific places to make entry sure

Wait: (V.14) hang around, stay, lingering

Stand thou not in the crossway: (v.14) junctions or intersections

Those of his that escape: (v.14) that speaks about escapees, deserters, apostates, traitors.

The day of Jehovah: (v.15) the judgment day for the world's nations and powers!

The Text
Obadiah 1: 10-16 ASV

[10] For the violence done to thy brother Jacob, shame shall cover thee, and thou shalt be cut off for ever.

[11] In the day that thou stoodest on the other side, in the day that strangers carried away his substance, and foreigners entered into his gates, and cast lots upon Jerusalem, even thou wast as one of them.

[12] But look not thou on the day of thy brother in the day of his disaster, and rejoice not over the children of Judah in the day of their destruction; neither speak proudly in the day of distress.

[13] Enter not into the gate of my people in the day of their calamity; yea, look not thou on their affliction in the day of their calamity, neither lay ye hands on their substance in the day of their calamity.

[14] And stand thou not in the crossway, to cut off those of his that escape; and deliver not up those of his that remain in the day of distress.

[15] For the day of Jehovah is near upon all the nations: as thou hast done, it shall be done unto thee; thy dealing shall return upon thine own head.

[16] For as ye have drunk upon my holy mountain, so shall all the nations drink continually; yea, they shall drink, and swallow down, and shall be as though they had not been.

Q3.1 How can you define violence? Especially how does violence work against blood brothers?

_____

_____

_____

_____

_____

Q3.2 How can you explain this reminder from the apostle James: "Whoever turns a sinner from the error of their way will save them from death and cover over a multitude of sins." (James 5:20)?

_____

_____

_____

_____

_____

Overview
"On the Day you stood aloof . . ."

No one has the power or ability to understand himself adequately unless he has the Holy Spirit! Thank God His Holy Spirit descended on Pentecost Sunday upon apostles and other believers from different nations.

Sorrowfully! This is not true with the Internationals or

people of other faiths, specifically the world of Islam. The unreached or Internationals cannot understand the mystery of God's grace because they do not have the power of the Holy Spirit! *"The person without the Spirit does not accept the things that come from the Spirit of God but considers them foolishness, and cannot understand them because they are discerned only through the Spirit."* (1 Corinthians 2:14 NIV)

In His presence, I want to challenge you to consider seriously who you are in His kingdom. What is your perception of yourself or others? We need to think thoughtfully; if we consider ourselves a part of His Kingdom, how are we playing our role as a kingdom person – on seeing Internationals, the unreached, and Gentiles? Do I recognize myself as a kingdom person?

Obadiah's book presents the conflict between Israel and Edom: Israel and Edom, the descendants of Abraham. The story is simple. God revealed to His prophet that Edom's destruction would occur because of her pride and alliance with Israel's adversaries.

"On the day you stood aloof . . . You should not gloat over your brother . . . in his misfortune" Obadiah 1:11-12

Have you ever considered where Islamic nations stand without knowing Jesus? What is their future? According to Lifeway statistics, they are on the way to becoming 2 billion people of the world population in the coming years.

As believers, we know God cares about them, and His heart

beats for the lost world of Islam.

What about you, "Do you care?"

What about us, "Do we care?"

Or, what about me, "Do I care?"

I'm bringing to your attention three points to figure out one question. . . where do we stand in response to this thoughtful question?

Or let me put it more personally to think deeply about why I stand aloof?

The straightforward truth and the challenging statement that Obadiah reveals and makes is, *"On the day you stood aloof . . ."*

What is THAT DAY? This day speaks about each day that we are living on this earth. I am not talking about what it means in the prophecy. My approach is simple and straightforward. THAT DAY actually is every day of my life till my Lord Jesus comes!

Every day I live on this earth reflects the picture of THAT DAY! I believe the Living Word of God works every day.

What is it to "stand aloof?"

Standing aloof means:

- Showing disinterest and keeping oneself reserved,
- It is avoiding someone,

- It mirrors an arrogant attitude toward the lost brethren.

We may be good, loving, and charitable within the church family or our inner circles, but who we are when we are in outer circles of Christian friends, but who are we when we are in the outer circles, in the harvest field, at the marketplace, or the mall. How do we respond to seeing Internationals?

- Do we keep our distance?
- Do we consider ourselves superior in showing an attitude toward them?
- Or, do we approach them in Christly love?

Where are we standing with lost Internationals?

Aloof?

What attitude are we showing to them?

Indifferent?

Uncaring?

Unconcerned?

Are we friendly to them to talk back and forth to show how much Jesus loves them? And what did He do for them?

Q3.3 What was Edom's attitude toward his blood-related brethren?

_____

_____

_____

_____

_____

Q3.4 God spoke clearly in His Word, *"Do not gloat when your enemy falls; when they stumble, do not let your heart rejoice,"* (Proverbs 24:17)? Do you think Edomites were aware of it or not? Support your answer with reasoning.

_____

_____

_____

_____

_____

Q3.5 Going through verses 12 to 14, explain what Edom had done. What were they supposed to do, and yet, they didn't do?

_____

_____

_____

_____

_____

Q3.6 How can you explain the term "Standing aloof"? Are we are standing aloof in the matter of the Islamic world? Explain. Yes or no.

_____

_____

_____

_____

_____

Q3.7 Obadiah provides us with two days: the Day of Trouble and Misfortune (v.12-14) and the DAY OF THE LORD (v.15). How are these days different?

_____

_____

_____

_____

_____

Q3.8 The people who do not believe in Jesus' Lordship are living in a day of disaster. How does John 3:36 make this point?

_____

_____

_____

_____

_____

Love God Love People – is the descriptive diction of brotherly love. In Matthew 22 Jesus calls this the Great Commandment.

The Great Commandment is to love God and love People. Isn't this true? Love God and love people is what the Savior demands from His people. Our Lord wants us to see an accelerating momentum of brotherly love.

Prophet Obadiah used the term "Brother" to make clear how important they are . . . in God's view.

How Islamic people can be our brothers and sisters might pop up in our minds. It is not possible! There's no blood relationship with them.

That's true!

Why did the Savior shed His blood?

He shed His blood to reconcile nations. His precious blood cries out loudly in them and convinces us to believe they are our brothers and sisters. The Slain Lamb, with His blood, purchased men for God. (Revelation 5:9).

The Apostle Paul uses the word "Philadelphia" in his epistles to refer to the Gentiles.

Why?

The Greek word "Philadelphia" means love shared between biological brothers and sisters.

"How would I dare to call her sister?" was a question posed to me in NY by a sister in Christ. I answered her, "Because of Jesus' Royal blood!"

We need to reach nations, the internationals, and the unreached people. They are Abraham's children and dear to us. We can't ignore them; we know they are lost brothers and sisters, and we are supposed to bring them into the Father's House! Though they deny the Lordship of Jesus Christ, we should still approach them and not overlook them! They are brethren and are in a miserable situation.

God says, *"If I am a Master where is the respect due Me?" (Malachi 1:6 NIV).* God says, "If I am your Master why don't you show respect to Me?"

Think about, how many hours, or days in a week or a month we have taken His Great Commission seriously? Aren't we standing aloof? Can we think deeply about living differently to give God glory according to His purposes? God cares; do I?

Obadiah declares, *"On the day you stood aloof . . . in the day of his misfortune"* [] (Obadiah 1:11-12). What is our situation having Internationals amongst us?

Isn't this true? Without knowing Jesus, people are living *"in the day of their misfortune."* Our worldly perspective inspires us to believe that people are in a miserable situation when they are hungry, thirsty, without medicine, illiterate, and without a place to live, naked, or wearing tattered clothing.

Let me tell you straightforwardly; if people are hungry or thirsty, or wounded or naked or illiterate, it would be the smallest misfortune compared to the loss of the joy of dwelling for eternity with Christ!

The people are in more significant trouble if they are not aware of the saving knowledge of Christ. We need to keep our eyes on the fact that they will not only suffer and be away from His sweet presence but also spend eternity in hell.

Trust me, if we are not reaching them to redeem them from the clutches of the Adversary, we are standing aloof and showing callousness and insensitivity. It is written in the Word of God; *"And should I not have concern for the great city of Nineveh, in which there are more than a hundred and twenty thousand people who cannot tell their right hand from their left - - and also so many animals?"* (John 4:11 NIV)

What do you think: The God who cares for animals does not care for internationals? How is it possible? It is beyond Him!

We are the custodians of His Supreme, the Holy, and the Final Revelation. We are His Word keepers; we are supposed to open our lips for the lost, uplifting interceding prayers. Or, otherwise, we could be blamed! We will be accountable for the lost on the LORD's Day.

God says, "If then I Am a Father where is my honor?

"Where is the honor due Me?'

"Why don't you honor Me?"(Malachi 1:6).

God cares, so He says:

It would be best if you did not gloat over your brethren . . .in the day of their disaster.

It would be best if you did not march through their gates . . .in the day of their calamity.

You should not wait at the crossroads . . . go ahead, go faster in love to show Jesus' love, His matchless grace, and His supreme sacrifice.

A Link to Islam

The Brotherhood: Esau's pride and hatred toward Israel vs. the Church's pride and hatred toward the people of the Crescent (the people of the Muslim faith)

The brotherhood is another parallel that is noticeable in the Book of Obadiah. Islamic people believe in the brotherhood. And they believe in this strongly! And their ideology is deep and vast concerning brotherhood.

Dr. Iqbal – one of the Islamic poets, entrusted his worldview concerning the brotherhood of Islamic people in such a way:

Our heart does not belong to India, Rum (Turkey) or Syria;
Our only habitation is Islam.

He says in his collection of poems known as ***Asrar-o-Rumuz***
–
We bail from Hejaz, China, Iran,
We are the dews of the same smiling morn.

He speaks to the Islamic world keeping in view a quite amazing, and revolutionary approach:

Break all idols of colour and blood and merge yourself into millat,

Because the Turonian, Iranians, and Afghans have lost their past glory.

For Iqbal, the word *"Millat"* is deep and profound. He expresses that Islamic people are not Turonian, Iranian, or Afghans. Instead, they are one Millat – one nation under the banner of Islam. The color, race, or blood does not matter, but the religion – Islam.

We know Esau showed pride and hatred toward Israel, and without any exaggeration; the church in general is preyed to pride and hatred. Her attitude is like Edomites showing no concern for Islamic people.

Though the Islamic people seem to us strangers and outsiders. They are not.

Being lost, they are a challenge to us.

And at the same time, they are dear to us, for Christ's sake!!

My Christian DNA inspires me to be in link with them. It provided me with a challenge to develop in relational brotherhood.

It accelerates my feet to run toward them zealously to show them Christly love! Even though I cannot find any genuine reason to be in link with them, I must take a risk to make a link for my Lord!

YHVH remembers internationals – they are his belonging; they are not far or aloof. Therefore, He is interested in them.

PLEASE REMEMBER!!!! No one is beyond His reach.

Therefore, being indifferent, uninterested, or unconcerned toward them is not wise! He remembers them because He is a covenant-keeping God. God invested a lot! He sacrificed His precious Son!

He declares through His prophet Isaiah, *"All the flock of Kedar shall be gathered together to you, The rams of Nebaioth shall minister to you; They shall ascend with acceptance on My altar, And I will glorify the house of My glory."* [] (Isaiah 60:7 NKJV).

Truth is the lost internationals; the dwelling ethnicities in the world are sons and daughters of Abraham.

Are we ready to bring them into Jesus' flock? Please do not ignore them and say they are not brethren. They are in desperate need of getting saved.

Shall we keep standing aloof, showing no interest in their salvation? Do we dare to ignore our mandate to reach them in their misfortunate circumstances?

Do we behave like Edomites making accusations, charges, or allegations?

Edom was treating the Israelites as strangers. How do we treat Internationals? **We need to carefully consider that sin includes not only what we do but also what we refuse to do.**

Are we ignoring or refusing the needs of Internationals?

'The Apostle James says, *"anyone, then, who knows the good he ought to do and doesn't do it, sins."* (James 4:17).

A Few Verses to Dig Deeper into . . .

"Whoever mocks the poor shows contempt for their Maker; whoever gloats over disaster will not go unpunished" (Proverbs 17:5)

"If I have rejoiced at my enemy's misfortune or gloated over the trouble that came to him–" (Job 31:29)

"But when I stumbled, they gathered in glee; assailants gathered against me without my knowledge. They slandered me without ceasing." (Psalms 35:15)

"Do not let those gloat over me who are my enemies without cause; do not let those gloat over me who hate me without reason maliciously wink the eye." (Psalms 35:19)

"Do not gloat over me, my enemy! Though I have fallen, I will rise. Though I sit in darkness, the LORD will be my light." (Micah 7:8)

"Do not gloat when your enemy falls; when they stumble, do not let your heart rejoice," (Proverbs 24:17)

Q3.9 Does the Great Commandment have any impact if the Great Commission is not the finishing point?! Is our attitude toward Islam or the people of other faiths like Edom's? If so, how can we fulfill either the Great Commission or the Great Commandment?

_____

_____

_____

_____

_____

Q3.10 Would you feel any restlessness in your gut to see the lost ethnicities worldwide? What is your opinion that sin includes not only what we do but also what we refuse to do? (See James 4:17). Will we be accountable for lost people on Judgement Day?

_____

_____

_____

_____

_____

Q3.11 How can you show grace to lost internationals by obeying the Great Commandment and accelerating the flow of the Great Commission? God cares, do you?

_____

_____

_____

_____

_____

Personal Reflection: How should we pray in light of what you just studied this week?

_____

_____

_____

_____

_____

_____

How did God speak to you this week?

_____

_____

_____

_____

_____

_____

_____

_____

_____

_____

_____

_____

_____

_____

_____

_____

_____

_____

Challenging Scenario

Shall we keep standing aloof, showing no interest in Muslims' salvation? Do we dare to ignore our mandate to reach them in their unfortunate circumstances? If not, what approach would you like to adopt?

_____
_____
_____
_____
_____
_____
_____
_____
_____
_____
_____
_____
_____
_____
_____
_____
_____
_____
_____
_____
_____
_____

OBADIAH

Week 4: God's Declaration For the Nations

The Kingdom Will Be The LORD's

Week 4:

God – The Sovereign King

"And saviours shall come up on mount Zion to judge the mount of Esau; and the kingdom shall be Jehovah's."
Obadiah 1:21 (ASV)

Whoa! What a declaration! The Kingdom will be the LORD's! Because He is the Sovereign God. Everything is in the world under His Lordship and Kingship! There's no exception available; even the rejecters of faith have to bow down before Him one day.

Background Thoughts

What system plays a better role: Democracy or monarchy?
Give your opinion.

_____

_____

_____

_____

_____

Are we able to notice democratic glimpses throughout the
Holy Bible? What does the Holy Bible say about democracy
or monarchy?

_____

_____

_____

_____

_____

Insight on the Text

Mount Zion: (v.17) the dwelling place of YHVH God. (see the references: Isaiah 8:18; 24:23; Psalm 74:2).

There shall be those that escape: (v.17) this statement speaks about the remnants of nations. We are obliged to concede that there is no way to escape about 2 billion people of the Islamic world who are a part of Obadiah's prophecy about the remnant.

The South: (v.19a) the South or the southern part of Israel is known as the Negev Desert. Presently, not all of this Desert but most of this land is under Israel's boundaries. According to the Encyclopedia of Britannica, this hot and dry, Desert covers about 4,700 square miles.

The lowland: (v.19b) represents the people of the Philistines.

Saviours: (v.21) the deliverers, the emancipators.

The Text
Obadiah 1: 17-21 ASV

17 But in mount Zion there shall be those that escape, and it shall be holy; and the house of Jacob shall possess their possessions.

18 And the house of Jacob shall be a fire, and the house of Joseph a flame, and the house of Esau for stubble, and they shall burn among them, and devour them; and there shall not be any remaining to the house of Esau; for Jehovah hath spoken it.

¹⁹ *And they of the South shall possess the mount of Esau, and they of the lowland the Philistines; and they shall possess the field of Ephraim, and the field of Samaria; and Benjamin shall possess Gilead.*

²⁰ *And the captives of this host of the children of Israel, that are among the Canaanites, shall possess even unto Zarephath; and the captives of Jerusalem, that are in Sepharad, shall possess the cities of the South.*

²¹ *And saviours shall come up on mount Zion to judge the mount of Esau; and the kingdom shall be Jehovah's.*

Q4.1 What is your perspective on this statement, *"But in Mount Zion there shall be those that escape"*? What do you think are the people who escape?

_____

_____

_____

_____

_____

Q4.2 How would you differentiate between *"The remnant of Israel"* and *"The remnant of men"*? Do you consider Muslims a part of the remnant of men or not? Give reasons for your viewpoint.

_____

_____

_____

_____

_____

Overview
Of The Theology of "The Remnant"

Verses 17-21 externally speak about the Israelites' restoration. But the cognitive meanings of these verses take us from each person to the person in the world whose hearts have been engraved with the Master's name! Whoever has touched the taste of eternal life by believing in His Lordship! No matter what ethnicity or people group they belong to, if their minds, hearts, and consciences have been enlightened by Jesus' light and edified by His grace, no one can hinder their deliverance.

The Word of God declares, *"But in mount Zion there shall be those that escape, and it shall be holy; and the house of Jacob shall possess their possessions."* (v.17 ASV).

The word escape stands for evasion, deliverance, or getting away. Another fascinating and noteworthy implication of this word provides us with the reasoning of the meaning – "the Remnant."

The Apostle Paul quotes the Old Testament prophecy of the Prophet Isaiah that he delivered in Isaiah 10:22, 23. In his epistle to the Church of Rome, he writes: *"And Isaiah crieth concerning Israel, if the number of the children of Israel be as the sand of the sea, it is the remnant that will be saved: for the Lord will execute his word upon the earth, finishing it and cutting it short."*(Romans 9:27-28 ASV)

Paul preached by emphasizing the remnant of Israel, and the Prophet Obadiah, on the contrary, talks about the remnant of the nations of the world!

How can we say that the Prophet Obadiah speaks about the remnant of Gentiles?

Let me verify my point by referring to another prophecy from the minor Prophet named Amos.

He predicted very clearly in such a way:

"In that day "I will restore David's fallen shelter – I will repair its broken walls and restore its ruins– and will rebuild it as it used to be, so that they may possess the remnant of Edom and all the nations that bear my name, declares the LORD, who will do these things." (Amos 9:11-12 NIV)

What do you think? What does it mean, ***"the remnant of Edom and all the nations"***?

I believe this remnant talks about Edomites, Islamic ethnicities, and even all the nations of the world! Praise be to God the Father, who provided us with the glorious grace of our Lord Jesus.

The agreement between the two prophecies makes it clear that the theology of remnant is not only talking about God's Israel but God's Gentiles too!

In *the first church conference*, the Apostle James quotes the Prophet Amos' prophecy concerning the remnant and professes to declare, *"Brothers, listen to me. Simon has described to us how God at first showed his concern by taking from the Gentiles a people for himself. The words of the prophets are in agreement with this, as it is written,*

" 'After this I will return
  and rebuild David's fallen tent.
  its ruins I will rebuild,
  and I will restore it,
  that the remnant of men may seek the Lord,
  and all the Gentiles who bear my name,
  says the Lord, who does these things
  that have been known for ages." (Acts 15:13-18)

 In verse fifteen, Obadiah's message asserts, *"The Day of the LORD is near upon all the nations."*

Throughout the Holy Scriptures, The Day of the LORD stands for the Great Tribulation. Obadiah predicts the Great Tribulation! The time of the completion of this prophecy is not far. Trust me; it is at hand.

Q4.3 How can you explain "the Day of the LORD"? How does the theology of the remnant go with the Day of the LORD?

_____

_____

_____

_____

_____

Q4.4 What was the Apostle James' judgment concerning the Gentiles in the first church conference? (See Acts 15:19,20).

_____

_____

_____

_____

_____

Q4.5 How did Islam divide the world? How many houses are in the world, according to Muslim theologians?

_____

_____

_____

_____

_____

Q4.6 What is explained about Edom in Amos 9:11-12? How can you interpret it?

_____

_____

_____

_____

_____

Q4.7 Who are these "Saviours" that Obadiah has discussed?

_____

_____

_____

_____

_____

Q4.8 What is your perspective on *And saviours shall come up on mount Zion to judge the mount of Esau;*"(Obadiah 1:21 ASV)? What do you think about mount Zion and Esau's mount? What would be the criterion for judgment?

_____

_____

_____

_____

_____

A Link to Islam

Islam: The religion of "submission." The word Islam provides us with the meaning of submission. Another aspect of Islam mirrors it as totalitarian religion. Allah's Attributive name مَالِكُ الْمُلْكِ **"Malik Al-Malik," is another** parallel that helps us to see where our Islamic friends are standing with their ideology! That's the only reason you'll hear, Muslims feel pride to be called "Abd-Allah", which means "a slave of Allah."

One of Allah's Attributive Names, مَالِكُ الْمُلْكِ **"Malik Al-Malik,"** expresses Allah's Sovereignty, Dominion, and control over all and everything. He knows everything. There is nothing that is hidden from Allah! Such is His kingdom.

"The Day whereon they will (all) come forth: not a single thing concerning them is hidden from Allah. Whose will be the Dominion that Day?" that of Allah, the one, the Irresistible!"

(The Noble Quran, Surah, THE BELIEVER 40:16)

v.25"And among His Signs is this, that heaven and earth stand by His command: then when He calls you, by a single call, from the earth, behold, you (straightway) come forth. v.26. To Him belongs every being that is in the heavens and on earth: all are devoutly obedient to Him. v.27. It is He who begins (the process of) creation." (The Nobel Quran, Surah, THE ROMANS 30:25-27)

"Glory to Allah, the Lord of the Throne: (high is He) above what they attribute to Him!" (The Noble Quran, Surah THE POETS 21:36).

"See they not that We gradually reduce the land (in their control) from its outlying borders?" (The Noble Quran, Surah, THE THUNDER 13:41).

"Say: "O Allah! Lord of Power (and Rule), You give Power to whom You please, and You strip off Power from whom You please: You endue with honour whom You please, and You bring low whom You please: in Your hand is all Good. Surely over all things You have Power. . . You bring the Living out of the Dead, and You bring the Dead out of the Living; and You give sustenance to whom You please, without measure" (The Noble Quran, Surah, THE FAMILY OF 'IMRAN 3:26-27).

"So glory to Him in Whose hands is the dominion of all things."

(The Noble Quran Surah YA SIN 36:83).

"He directs (all) affairs from the heavens to the earth: . . ." (The Noble Quran Surah, THE PROSTRATION 32:5).

The Rise of The King & the Fall of Edomites and Other Nations:

In the Pentateuch, Balaam's final oracle concludes with the rise of the King and the fall of Edomites and other nations; revealing and declaring the rise of God's Kingdom:

v. 16. "He speaks, who heard the words of God and knew the knowledge of the Most High, who saw the vision of the Almighty, falling down, but having his eyes open and uncovered:
v.17. I see Him, but not now; I behold Him, but He is not near. A star(Star) shall come forth out of Jacob, and a scepter (Scepter) shall rise out of Israel and shall crush all the corners of Moab and break down all the sons of Sheth [Moab's sons of tumult].
v.18. And Edom shall be [taken as] possession, [Mount] Seir also shall be dispossessed, who were Israel's enemies, while Israel does valiantly. [] (Numbers 24:16-18).

The Apostle Matthew explains the shocking experience of the magi – the wise men of the East who came to Jerusalem seeing the star of the born king of the Jews.

They were inquiring in awe,

"Where is He Who has been born King of the Jews? For we have seen His star in the east at its rising and have come to worship

Him." [] (Matthew 2:2 AMPC) and references to Numbers 24:17; Jeremiah 23:5; Zechariah 9:9)

John Mark shows the crowning of the Masih King with a noticeable, modest, and humble approach in Injil Sharif Mark Chapter 7.
This coronation shows the exact picture that the Old Testament Prophet Zechariah has sketched.

v.9. "Rejoice greatly, O Daughter of Zion!
Shout aloud, O Daughter of Jerusalem!
Behold, your king comes to you; He is [uncompromisingly] just
and having salvation [triumphant and victorious], patient, meek,
lowly, and riding on a donkey, upon a colt, the foal of a donkey."
(Zechariah 9:9 AMPC)

He portrayed the setting of the zealous mob, which is inspired and thrilled by the presence of His kingdom! A rejoicing mob out of its self-conscious shout out loudly:

"Hosanna!"
"Blessed is he who comes in the name of the Lord!"
"Blessed is the coming kingdom of our father David!"
"Hosanna in the highest heaven!"

They were actually welcoming the king by keeping their Jewish traditions (see the royal salute of Israelites they offered to Jehu in 2 Kings 9:12-13.)

In Injil Sharif John 18:37, we see Pontius Pilate in great bewilderment. He spoke to Al Masih.

v. "Then you are a King? Jesus answered you say it! [You speak correctly!] For I am a King. [Certainly, I am A King!] This is why I was born, and for this I have come into the world, to bear witness to the Truth. Everyone who is of the Truth [who is a friend of the Truth, who belongs to the Truth] hears and listens to My voice."

Many people in the world are so confused about Jesus' authority and His power. They are messed up because their worldly intellect has influenced their worldview. They are not ready to recognize –

His Lordship!

His Kingship!

In Injil Sharif Revelation, John the Revelator declares:

v.14. "They will wage war against the Lamb, but the Lamb will triumph over them because he is Lord of lords and King of kings– and with him will be his called, chosen and faithful followers." (Injil Sharif Revelation 17:14)

The nations of the world and the lost people are ensnared in their vain and lying ideologies. Alas! The untrue, incorrect, and fallacious assumptions seem dear to them.

This compound Arabic word مَالِكُ الْمُلْكِ **"Malik Al-Malik** means The King of Kings!

Who is this King of kings?

The Word of God deliberately declares Jesus is:

- the King of kings!
- And, the Lord of lords!

Let's read Injil Sharif Revelation 19:13 & 16,

"v.13.He is dressed in a robe dipped in blood, and his name is the Word of God."

"v.16.On his robe and on His thigh he has this name written:

KING OF KINGS AND LORD OF LORDS"

It means Jesus Christ – Isa Al Masih has authority over the kings and governing authorities of the world.

Because He Himself is the:

KING OF KINGS AND LORD OF LORDS

His Supremacy is unique and adorable!

Another interesting aspect attached to it is this Jesus, through his act of sacrificial death and resurrection, made us to be his kingdom. We being Christians, reign with Isa Al Masih. We are special people with special privileges!

Our rights are extraordinary because of his grace and unbounded love!

John the Revelator explains our privileges in Injil Sharif Revelation 1:5-6

v.5. and from Jesus Christ, who is the faithful witness, the firstborn from the dead, and the ruler of kings of the earth.

To him who loves us and has freed us from our sins by his blood,

v.6. and has made us to be a kingdom and priests to serve his God and Father– to him be glory and power for ever and ever! Amen.

We notice the repetition of this in Injil Sharif Revelation 5:10,

You have made them to be a kingdom and priests to serve our God, and they will reign on the earth.

We notice the echo of it in Isaiah's wording:

And you will be called priests of the LORD, you will be named ministers of our God. (Isaiah 61:6)

Jesus declared in Injil Sharif Revelation

To the one who is victorious, I will give the right to sit with me on my throne, just as I was victorious and sat down with my Father on his throne. (Injil Sharif Revelation 3:21)

Why is there reverberation of this thought that His people will be priests and ministers and reign with Isa Al Masih?

Why?

How can our Muslim friends believe in this? Do they find any clue about Jesus' Kingdom and the privileges of His devotes?

Are there any signs available in the Noble Quran concerning these things?

These are very reasonable questions, and we need to address

them intelligently and sensibly!

Keeping in view judicious, rational, and intellectual approaches and respecting their mindset, we need to provide them with reasoning from the Noble Quran.

The Noble Quran says about Isa's (Jesus') devotees,

"I will make those who follow you superior to those who reject faith, to the Day of Resurrection." (The Noble Quran, Surah, Al-'Imran 3: 55)

Q4.9 Can we dare to share with them who is mine, King? And what did He do for me?

_____

_____

_____

_____

_____

Q4.10 How can we use the references from the Noble Quran to help our Muslim friends be convinced of the Kingship of our Lord Jesus Christ?

_____

_____

_____

_____

_____

Q4.11 What are the privileges of Christians being Isa Al Masih's devotees? What is the expanse of their set privileges according to the Noble Quran?

_____

_____

_____

_____

_____

Personal Reflection: How should we pray in light of what you just studied this week?

_____

_____

_____

_____

_____

_____

How did God speak to you this week?

_____

_____

_____

_____

_____

_____

_____

_____

_____

Challenging Scenario

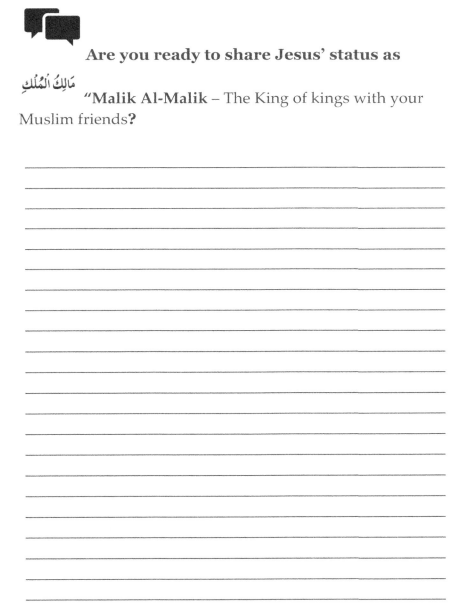

Are you ready to share Jesus' status as

مَالِكُ الْمُلْكِ

"Malik Al-Malik – The King of kings with your Muslim friends?

_____
_____
_____
_____
_____
_____
_____
_____
_____
_____
_____
_____
_____
_____
_____
_____
_____
_____
_____
_____
_____
_____
_____
_____

Appendix (A)

Sahih Al-Bukhari 4:583 (The Narration of Ibn 'Abbas)

The first lady to use a girdle was the mother of Ishmael. She used a girdle so that she might hide her tracks from Sarah. Abraham brought her and her son Ishmael while she was suckling him, to a place near the Kaaba under a tree on the spot of Zam-zam, at the highest place in the mosque. During those days there was nobody in Mecca, nor was there any water. So he made them sit over there and placed near them a leather bag containing some dates, and a small water-skin containing some water, and set out homeward. Ishmael's mother followed him saying, 'O Abraham! Where are you going, leaving us in this valley where there is no person whose company we may enjoy, nor is there anything (to enjoy)?' She repeated that to him many times, but he did not look back at her. Then she asked him, 'Has Allah ordered you to do so?'

He said, 'Yes.'

She said, 'Then He will not neglect us,' and returned while Abraham proceeded onwards.

Upon reaching the Thaniya where they could not see him, he faced the Kaaba, and raising both hands, invoked Allah saying the following prayers, 'O our Lord! I have made some of my offspring dwell in a valley without cultivation, by Your Sacred House (Kaaba at Mecca) in order, O our Lord, that they may offer prayer perfectly. So fill some hearts among men with love towards them, and (O Allah) provide them with fruits, so that they may give thanks.' (14.37) Ishmael's mother went on suckling Ishmael and drinking from the water (she had).

When the water in the water-skin had all been used up, she became thirsty and her child also became thirsty. She started looking at him (Ishmael) tossing in agony. She left him, for she could not endure looking at him, and found that the mountain of Safa was the nearest mountain to her on that land. She stood on it and started looking at the valley keenly so that she might see somebody, but she could not see anybody. Then she descended from Safa and when she reached the valley, she tucked up her robe and ran in the valley like a person in distress and trouble, until she crossed the valley and reached Marwa Mountain where she stood and started looking, expecting to see somebody, but she could not see anybody. She repeated that (running between Safa and Marwa) seven times.

The Prophet said, "This is the source of the tradition of the walking of people between them (i.e. Safa and Marwa)."

When she reached Marwa (for the last time) she heard a voice and she asked herself to be quiet and listened attentively. She heard the voice again and said, 'O, (whoever you may be)! You have made me hear your voice; have you got something to help me?' And behold! She saw an angel at the place of Zam-zam, digging the earth with his heel (or his wing), until water flowed from that place. She started to make something like a basin around it, using her hand in this way, and started filling her water-skin with water with her hands, and the water was flowing out after she had scooped some of it.

The Prophet added, "May Allah bestow Mercy on Ishmael's mother! Had she let the Zam-zam (flow without trying to control it) (or had she not scooped from that water to fill her water-skin), Zam-zam would have been a stream flowing on the surface of the earth."

The Prophet further added, "Then she drank (water) and suckled her child. The angel said to her, 'Don't be afraid of being neglected, for this is the House of Allah which will be built by this boy and his father, and Allah never neglects His people.'"

The House (i.e. Kaaba) at that time was on a high place resembling a hillock, and when torrents came, they flowed to its right and left. She lived in that way until some people from the tribe of Jurhum or a family from Jurhum passed by her and her child, as they (i.e. the Jurhum people) were coming through the way of Kaaba. They landed in the lower part of Mecca where they saw a bird that had the habit of flying around water and not leaving it. They said, 'This bird must be flying around water, though we know that there is no water in this valley.' They sent one or two messengers who discovered the source of water, and returned to inform them of the water. So, they all came (towards the water).

The Prophet added, "Ishmael's mother was sitting near the water. They asked her, 'Do you allow us to stay with you?'

"She replied, 'Yes, but you will have no right to possess the water.'

"They agreed to that."

The Prophet further said, "Ishmael's mother was

pleased with the whole situation as she used to love to enjoy the company of the people."

So, they settled there, and later on they sent for their families who came and settled with them so that some families became permanent residents there. The child (Ishmael) grew up and learned Arabic from them and (his virtues) caused them to love and admire him as he grew up, and when he reached the age of puberty they made him marry a woman from among them.

After Ishmael's mother had died, Abraham came after Ishmael's marriage in order to see his family that he had left before, but he did not find Ishmael there. When he asked Ishmael's wife about him, she replied, 'He has gone in search of our livelihood.'

Then he asked her about their way of living and their condition, and she replied, 'We are living in misery; we are living in hardship and destitution,' complaining to him.

He said, 'When your husband returns, convey my salutation to him and tell him to change the threshold of the gate (of his house).'

When Ishmael came, he seemed to have felt something unusual, so he asked his wife, 'Has anyone visited you?'

She replied, 'Yes, an old man of so-and-so description came and asked me about you and I informed him, and he asked about our state of living, and I told him that we were living in hardship and poverty.'

On that Ishmael said, 'Did he advise you anything?'

She replied, 'Yes, he told me to convey his salutation to you and to tell you to change the threshold of your gate.'

Ishmael said, 'It was my father, and he has ordered me to divorce you. Go back to your family.' So, Ishmael divorced her and married another woman from amongst them (i.e. Jurhum).

Then Abraham stayed away from them for a period as long as Allah wished and called on them again but did not find Ishmael. So he came to Ishmael's wife and asked her about Ishmael. She said, 'He has gone in search of our livelihood.'

Abraham asked her, 'How are you getting on?' asking her about their sustenance and living.

She replied, 'We are prosperous and well-off (i.e. we have everything in abundance).' Then she thanked Allah.

Abraham said, 'What kind of food do you eat?' She said, 'Meat.'

He said, 'What do you drink?'

She said, 'Water.'

He said, "O Allah! Bless their meat and water."

The Prophet added, "At that time they did not have grain, and if they had grain, he would have also invoked Allah to bless it." The Prophet added, "If somebody has only these two things as his sustenance, his health and disposition will be badly affected, unless he lives in Mecca."

Then Abraham said to Ishmael's wife, 'When your husband comes, give my regards to him and tell him that he should keep firm the threshold of his gate.'

When Ishmael came back, he asked his wife, 'Did anyone call on you?'

She replied, 'Yes, a good-looking old man came to me,' so she praised him and added. 'He asked about you, and I informed him, and he asked about our livelihood and I told him that we were in a good condition.'

Ishmael asked her, 'Did he give you any piece of advice?'

She said, 'Yes, he told me to give his regards to you and ordered that you should keep firm the threshold of your gate.'

On that Ishmael said, 'It was my father, and you are the threshold (of the gate). He has ordered me to keep you with me.'

Then Abraham stayed away from them for a period as long as Allah wished, and called on them afterwards. He saw Ishmael under a tree near Zam-zam, sharpening his arrows. When he saw Abraham, he rose up to welcome him (and they greeted each other as a father does with his son or a son does with his father). Abraham said, 'O Ishmael! Allah has given me an order.'

Ishmael said, 'Do what your Lord has ordered you to do.'

Abraham asked, 'Will you help me?'

Ishmael said, 'I will help you.'

Abraham said, 'Allah has ordered me to build a house here,' pointing to a hillock higher than the land surrounding it.

The Prophet added, "Then they raised the foundations of the House (i.e. the Kaaba). Ishmael brought the stones and Abraham was building, and when the walls became high, Ishmael brought this stone and put it for Abraham who stood over it and carried on building, while

Ishmael was handing him the stones, and both of them were saying, 'O our Lord! Accept (this service) from us. Verily, You are the All-Hearing, the All-Knowing.' The Prophet added, "Then both of them went on building and going round the Kaaba saying: 'O our Lord! Accept (this service) from us. Verily, You are the All-Hearing, the All-Knowing.'" (2.127)

APPENDIX (B)

Overview of Islamic Beliefs

1. Belief in God "Allah"

Islamic friends believe in God. And they used the specific name for God that is known as "Allah."[] They believe Allah is the only and one true God. The term 'Allah' is propbably derived from al-illah, which means the god. Allah is all-seeing, all speaking, all-knowing, all-willing, and all-powerful. Allah is not trinity; He is one and alone. They do believe Allah has ninety-nine attributive names known as "Al-Asma Al-Husna" means the most beautiful names of Allah. Each of these names reflects the glory of Almighty God. Interestingly, all these attributive names or "Al-Asma Al-Husna are matched with the YWAH God of the Bible.

2. Belief in angels

Muslims believe in the hierarchy of angels, the chief of whom is Jibril (Gabriel), who consecutively brought to Muhammad the revelations of Allah (Surah 2:97). Muslims also believe that Gabriel is the Holy Spirit of Christianity. There is another major angel, Israfel, who will play the trumpet on the last day to gather all the dead of the world. Each person has two recording angels who list up a person's good and bad deeds (Surah 50:17). This recorded history will be provided to Allah on the day of resurrection.

3. Belief in the messengers or prophets

There are 124,000 prophets who have been sent to human beings throughout history. Each prophet came with a truth for a specific period of time with a special message to his people. Adam was the first prophet of Allah. Other prominent prophets are Noah, Abraham, Moses, David,

Solomon, Jonah, John the Baptist, and Jesus. However, Muhammad is the last and the most prominent messenger of Allah, as he is the prophet for all time. He is the seal of the prophets.

4. Belief in the heavenly books

Muslims believe four books have come down or descended to earth from heaven. They regard these as Holy or Heavenly Books. They are the Torah (the Books of Moses, or the Old Testament), Zabur (Psalms), Injil (the Gospel or the New Testament), and the Quran. According to Islam, the older three books have been corrupted by Jews and Christians and are no longer reliable.

5. Belief in a judgment day

Muslims believe in a Judgment Day. Allah, who observes all people's deeds, will make the decision as a judge weighing someone's deeds whether the person is eligible for Paradise (a place of pleasure) or Hell (a place of eternal torment).

6. Belief in fate

Believing in fate or predestination is another basic belief. Muslims believe everything is foreordained by Allah, which means everything is already arranged or determined in advance before it happens.

There are Five or Six obligations or practices that are known as pillars of Islam

1. Shahada

Shahada is *the confession of faith*, expressing that one believes in his or her heart that there is no god but Allah and Muhammad is His prophet. It is the Muslim creed. Shahada consists of two fundamental beliefs:

"La ilaha illa Allah wa Muhammad Rasul Allah."

It means, "There is no god but Allah, and Muhammad is His prophet."

The recitation of these words in front of two Muslim witnesses makes someone Muslim.

When is the Shahada recited?

- Shahada is recited in the *Izan* time, when the *Muezzin* calls Muslims to prayer.
- It is also a part of five-times-a-day *Salat* (prayer)
- Even Sufis (members of a sect of Islam) recite the Shahada in their meditative praying times.

Shahada in Shi'a Islam:

In Shi'a Islam, the Shahada declaration is lengthened with the addition of a phrase concerning Ali, the Fourth Caliph of Islam. "*Wa Aliyun waliyyu l-Lah.*" The word *wali* means *friend*.

2. Salat

Salat is an Arabic word for *prayer*. Muslims are commanded to pray in a prescribed way five times every day. From a high tower on a mosque, a Muezzin sings an invitation to all in a city to pray at these specific times. These daily prayers are named by the time of day they occur.

1. Fajr   (at dawn)
2. Dhuhr   (at noon)
3. Asr   (in the afternoon)
4. Maghrib   (at sunset)
5. Isha'a   (at night)

3. Saum

Saum means *fasting*. The month of Ramadan is dedicated to fasting. Each day, the fast begins at dawn and ends at dusk. Food and drink may be enjoyed before dawn and after sunset. There are many devotional activities which take place during this month as well.

Because the normal day is disrupted with a fast, a special meal is prepared before dawn. This meal is *Suhur*. Another meal is prepared after sunset called *Iftar*. Usually, people break their fast with a few dates and a cup of water, and then the other meal things are served.

4. Zakat

Zakat is *almsgiving*. Every Muslim must give 2.5% of his income based on his nonessential property. Zakat money is used to build *mosques* (places of worship of Allah) and *madrasas* (Islamic religious schools), to help needy persons, and to support the supreme cause of *Jihad* (Holy War).

5. Hajj

A *Hajj*, a p*ilgrimage to Mecca,* is required of every Muslim man. He must visit Mecca in Saudi Arabia at least once in his lifetime to go to see the birthplace of the Prophet Muhammad. This journey takes place in the month of Dhu al-Hijjah, the twelfth month of the Islamic lunar calendar. Hajj can be performed either for oneself or for the sake of another person who is unable to it do for specified reasons. A Hajj is an intention to go to Mecca to perform specific acts. The first place of worship appointed by Allah *(masjid)* is the *Kaaba,* the Sacred House. Worshippers in the Sacred Mosque pray in concentric circles around the Kaaba. The Kaaba thus serves to unify Muslims all over the world.

OBADIAH

Ishmael's Call Announces

The release of Dr. Sadiq's new book

JONAH

Most people have heard of Jonah, but many have never considered how this 3,000-year- old story still impacts the world's two largest religions - Christianity and Islam.

- In this 4-week study, you will learn what message it contains for the people of Crescent?
- Why did God command Jonah to go to Nineveh?
- Why did He call Nineveh "the great city?" Why did God choose Jonah to speak as a prophet both to Israelites as well as Gentiles?
- Why did Jonah reject his God-given mandate?

Jonah's book is simple and straightforward, a plain message without confusion. It exposes God's heart for His lost creation. The story is appealing, it catches our imagination and delights a child's heart. But, in fact, it is not just a story, it is the true message of YHWH God who is faithful and whose heart beats for the nations. **S. Lance** *available to buy on Amazon*."

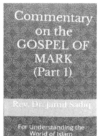

Commentary on
The GOSPEL OF MARK
For Understanding the World of Islam

Generally, Islam is that mission field, which is ignored by the church at large in the past. Even nowadays, we didn't find any earnest, serious, or solemn strategy that has been developed or adopted by the church at large to approach these beloved lost. We are not able to see any special excitement or thrill for reaching them. The church, fellow believers, and the congregants are slow to show some positive concern or interest that this group demands, needs, and deserves.

Can you believe that Islamic people have the same mindset as the Markan audience? Jesus Christ of Christianity is known as Messiah, and some others use the term, **Al Masih.** Isa Al Masih is the name mentioned in the Noble Quran (Surah 3), so this is popular amongst Islamic folks. You will be surprised to know that Islam, one of the world's largest religions, believes in Isa Al Masih's Prophethood. They consider Isa Al Masih one of the most noticeable, famous, and prominent prophets but deny the Deity of Isa Al Masih.

The purpose of this study is to prepare the followers of Jesus Christ, so they would be able to approach the people of other faiths, specifically the Islamic Umma (nation), by keeping in view the goal of helping them to remove their misconceptions about the Deity of Isa Al Masih.
Available on Amazon   ISBN **979-8853009202**

OBADIAH

OBADIAH

OBADIAH

OBADIAH

OBADIAH

OBADIAH

OBADIAH

OBADIAH

OBADIAH

Made in the USA
Las Vegas, NV
26 September 2023

78147123R00066